The Stewardship Series 2

WHERE YOUR TREASURE IS

Your Attitude About Finances

The Stewardship Series 2

WHERE YOUR TREASURE IS

Your Attitude About Finances

LARRY BURKETT

Edited and Arranged by Karen C. Lee-Thorp

© 1996 by
LARRY BURKETT

All rights reserved. No part of this book may be reproduced in any form without permission in writing from the publisher, except in the case of brief quotations embodied in critical articles or reviews.

All Scripture quotations are taken from the *Holy Bible, New International Version*.® NIV.® Copyright © 1973, 1978, 1984 International Bible Society. Used by permission of Zondervan Publishing House. All rights reserved.

Scripture quotations marked (NASB) are taken from the *New American Standard Bible*, © 1960, 1962, 1963, 1968, 1971, 1972, 1973, 1975, and 1977 by the Lockman Foundation, and are used by permission.

Edited by Adeline Griffith, Christian Financial Concepts

ISBN: 0-8024-2804-5

1 3 5 7 9 10 8 6 4 2

Printed in the United States of America

TABLE OF CONTENTS

USING THIS STUDY GUIDE

Learning to handle money and possessions is one of the most important things we can do for our spiritual growth. Our use of money both reflects and greatly affects the true state of our relationship with God. But money is a touchy subject—rarely discussed in pulpits or even in small groups—so many people are simply unaware of how much insight the Bible offers into handling money wisely.

The Stewardship Series of study guides is designed to help you learn and practice the basic biblical principles of handling wealth, whether you have a lot or a little. A *steward* is someone who manages another person's property; God has entrusted every one of us with resources to manage for His purposes. When we understand God's goals and methods, managing money can become an exciting adventure instead of a confusing burden.

Where Your Treasure Is addresses the foundational attitudes that drive our thoughts and feelings about money. By the end of these eight sessions, you may never look at your checkbook the same way. You'll discover some surprising things about yourself and catch a vision that goes far beyond just making ends meet.

First of all, this guide is designed with small groups in mind. Money is an intensely private matter, and you won't be asked to divulge information inappropriately, but teaming up with a group of like-minded people offers you the chance to learn from others and receive their encouragement. However, you can easily adapt *Where Your Treasure Is* for use with just one other person or even use it on your own. If you are helping someone else learn to manage his or her finances, you may find the guides in this series to be a helpful part of what you do together. Engaged and married couples also will find these guides invaluable in sorting out how to handle their finances jointly.

The following elements are included in the sessions.

Approach Question(s). Most sessions begin with one or two questions that invite participants to share what they've been thinking and feeling about money during the week. These questions often refer to the homework assignment from the previous session. Group members have a chance to share with each other what they have learned from the homework exercise.

Teaching and Scripture. Next there are several pages of teaching on a topic, built around a few key passages of Scripture. Ideally, participants should have read and digested this section before coming to the group meeting; but, the text is brief enough to take ten minutes to read it during the meeting. Key paragraphs and Scripture passages could be reread during the meeting in order to discuss the questions.

Discussion Questions. These questions invite you to respond to the teaching and Scripture. Two people probably could cover them in twenty minutes; eight or ten people could use an hour, although forty minutes would be adequate. Some questions may provoke such a lively discussion that the leader will have to decide whether to cut off the discussion and move on or skip some of the later questions. When a question is personal, you always have the option of writing a full answer on your own and telling the group only what you feel is appropriate.

The Grace Adventure. Each session closes with a reminder that God's grace is available to accomplish what God's Word asks of us. God doesn't issue a lot of commands and leave us to fend for ourselves. This section also includes a suggestion for how to pray in response to what you've been discussing. Prayer is a way of acknowledging and seeking God's grace.

If your group is accustomed to praying together, you may not need the suggestions to guide your prayers. If some participants are unaccustomed to praying aloud, you may decide to either make your prayer time brief, allow time for silent prayer only, or let some pray aloud and others remain silent. Decide on the ground rules for group prayer at your first meeting so no one will fear being put on the spot later on.

During the Week. A Bible study guide typically asks you to study one or more Bible passages in preparation for your next group meeting. By contrast, this guide asks you to reflect on one or two of the verses you have just discussed. The idea is to let the truths of those passages sink into your mind and heart.

You'll also be asked to pay attention to the way you handle money during the week, in light of what you have been discussing. Meditating on Scripture and observing your own behavior work together to help you really listen to what God is telling you to do.

Finally, you'll be asked to read the theme for the next session. If you only have time to either read the next session or do the other homework activities, choose the meditating and observing. However, reading ahead should take you only about ten minutes and will save a lot of time during your group meeting.

I trust that the Holy Spirit will guide you to examine your financial life through the teaching of God's Word.

* * * *

"Delight yourself in the Lord; and He will give you the desires of your heart. Commit your way to the Lord, trust also in Him, and He will do it. And He will bring forth your righteousness as the light, and your judgment as the noonday" (Psalm 37: 4–6 NASB).

"Now for this very reason also, applying all diligence, in your faith supply moral excellence, and in your moral excellence, knowledge; and in your knowledge, self-control, and in your self-control, perseverance, and in your perseverance, godliness; and in your godliness, brotherly kindness, and in your brotherly kindness, love. For if these qualities are yours and are increasing, they render you neither useless nor unfruitful in the true knowledge of our Lord Jesus Christ" (2 Peter 1:5–6 NASB).

Session 1

THE POWER OF MONEY

A Power Tool

Many people think the Bible says money is the root of all evil. Instead, it says, "*For the* **love** *of money is a root of all sorts of evil, and some by longing for it have wandered away from the faith, and pierced themselves with many a pang*" (1 Timothy 6:10 NASB, emphasis added). Money was created as a tool, as a medium of exchange to simplify life. It enabled a farmer to carry some of his wealth in his pocket and not have to carry around bushels of grain to swap for cloth and lumber.

However, we should never underestimate money's power just because it is a mere tool. In the 1940s, a device to split an atom and produce a nuclear reaction was invented as a tool with the potential to provide either enormous power to fuel factories and homes or the power to devastate the planet. Money is at least as powerful a tool and requires similar care in handling.

Money offers enormous power to the one who possesses it. It can buy survival, comfort, security, sex, allegiance, status, political office—the list is endless. If you've ever lived in financial uncertainty, not knowing from day to day whether you would be able to pay your bills, then you know how easily money can control your emotions and decisions. Money is one of the chief causes of strife within marriages, and conflict over money is a leading cause of divorce.

The powers of darkness have not failed to notice money's power, and these powers have centuries of experience in using money as a tool to destroy families and nations. In fact, when Jesus spoke about money, He often used the Aramaic term *mammon* to signify money's potential to become a god.

"No one can serve two masters; for either he will hate the one and love the other, or he will hold to one and despise the other. You cannot serve God and mammon" (Matthew 6:24 NASB).

The tide of the world sweeps us in the direction of bowing before money, letting it rule our lives. Money has been a potent god in many cultures, but in ours it has reached virtual supremacy. A bumper sticker parodies Descartes' famous statement of his philosophy: "I think, therefore I am." The bumper sticker reads, "I Shop, Therefore I Am." It is the creed of a nation whose cathedrals are huge malls with waterfalls, entertainment, salons, exercise clubs, banks—everything a modern consumer needs for a fulfilling life.

It is common practice now for inner-city teenagers to murder one another for leather jackets or the latest basketball shoes. In suburbia, parents hold two jobs to afford the right toys and the right clothes for their children, lest their children be labeled uncool, out of it, or outsiders in a culture where belonging is defined by what they own.

We decry gang violence and childhood materialism, but our youth have merely learned what we teach them on television, on billboards, and by our own habits. To own something is to have value; not to own is to be worthless. If you want something, you have a right to have it now, no money down, no interest for three months; worry about the payments later.

When consumer spending increases, Wall Street cheers, because spending is what drives our economy, and being "consumers" is our chief identity. Years ago, when a family could count on its standard of living rising year by year, mammon seemed a benign god. But now, when wages barely rise, just staying even is a struggle, and the pressure for new clothes, better cars, and more software, CDs, and videos is intolerable.

What can we do in the face of this pressure? Only a persistent commitment to know and do what God says about money will enable us to mold money into a tool to advance God's agenda instead of our own.

1. Can you identify with the pressure to consume? How have you experienced it recently?

____

____

____

____

2. Recount a time—perhaps from your childhood, a recent personal experience, or a story on the news—when you saw money's power control a person who didn't know how to control it.

3. Think about Matthew 6:24. Why is it impossible to serve both God and money?

Your Story

Money grips most of us at heart level, in emotions and values we rarely think about consciously. Some of those values come from significant experiences. For instance, Jan's parents lived poor and died poor; Jan dreads lacking money and dying penniless. She is deeply committed not to suffer what her parents suffered and not to put her children through what she went through as a child.

By contrast, twenty-three-year-old Bryan grew up in a reasonably affluent suburban home and attended college. He was shocked and angry when his first job didn't begin to pay for the lifestyle to which he was accustomed. Feeling entitled to his standard of living, he let his credit card bills mount.

David watched what happened when his parents

failed, and he learned to fear failure.

Gretchen, however, grew up with parents who were so engrossed in succeeding in their careers that they never had time for her. Gretchen learned to fear success.

Bill has known several Christians who applied what they thought was biblical teaching about money in absurd ways, so he fears he may ruin his own life if he takes biblical teaching seriously.

Other attitudes about money may be generational. Carl and Luci—born in the 1930s and raised during the Great Depression and World War II—were weaned on rationing, salvaging, and delayed gratification. Their children, born and raised in the years of rising expectations in the 50s and early 60s (the baby boom), were taught to work hard and get ahead so that the god mammon would bless them. Baby boomers tend to be hard workers who view upward mobility as a right and a mark of status.

On the other hand, men and women born after 1963 more often view climbing the ladder of success with cynicism. They know they're unlikely to be richer than their parents, and they don't see that money made them happy. They see money less as a status symbol than as a ticket to fun, a chance to live creatively instead of grinding out their days in monotony. And while baby boomers chafe at delayed gratification, few people under thirty today believe in it at all. Why should they expect tomorrow to be better than today?

Still other attitudes about money seem to be inborn. For men, money often represents the power to gain status and the symbols of status. Status means respect from other men (and respect is very important to men), and it also means attention from desirable women. Studies in cultures around the world show that women prefer to marry men with high status and lots of material resources.

Finally, money helps men feel that they are having a significant effect on their world. Their work matters if they are well paid for it, and the more money they have the more able they are to finance their projects. One of those projects is providing for a family. Men tend to feel much better about themselves as men when they succeed in providing for a family. Losing a job often devastates a man's self-esteem, because work and the resources work produces are so much a part of his identity. (These generalizations hold truer for men over thirty who are at or above an average middle-class income.)

By contrast, for women money traditionally represents security. Women seem to have an instinct to build a nest and enlist a man's support in raising children in that nest. Women today also are well aware that the likelihood of having to raise their children without a man is increasing. Money in the bank is the guarantee that a woman's family will be adequately supplied. Consequently, women tend to fear indebtedness more than men, who are more willing to gamble.

There are certainly many women today who are not planning to find husbands and raise children and who are primarily invested in their careers. Society tends to expect career women to spend much more on their appearance—clothing, jewelry, and grooming—than it expects men of equal incomes to spend. Men tend to feel more pressure to drive the right car.

It may be true that women buy on impulse more often than men, but when a woman spends impulsively, she will typically buy a new outfit. When a man takes the plunge, he will come home with a new car or boat. Men spend less often, but when they do they spend more money.

Naturally, these generalizations have many exceptions, but I offer them here to help you begin thinking about your own feelings and beliefs about money and your spending habits.

Now take five to fifteen minutes, depending on how much time you have or need, to answer questions 4 through 8 privately.

4. What did you learn about money as a child from watching your father and/or mother? Check one or more of the following.

   - ❑ I determined never to be poor like they were.
   - ❑ I wanted to become as generous as they were.
   - ❑ I learned to view new-model cars, electronics, and housing as necessities, not luxuries.
   - ❑ I came to dislike the whole subject of money because it produced nothing but conflict in our home.
   - ❑ I learned to fear money as something that could take over a person's life because my father cared more about making money than about spending time with me.
   - ❑ My mother worried about money compulsively. I refuse to worry all the time about whether I'll have enough this month to pay my bills.

- ❑ I became comfortable with simple living.
- ❑ I learned to be grateful to God for the way He provided for us.
- ❑ Other (Describe your experience.)

5. a. In what ways do you identify with what is said above about the way men view money (if you are a man) or the way women view money (if you are a woman)?

   b. In what ways do you not identify with these generalizations?

6. What about the generational differences? Do those broad generalizations fit you at all?

7. Check any of the following that describe you.

- ❑ A compulsive saver
- ❑ Frugal by nature
- ❑ A person with a budget built into my brain
- ❑ Someone who views frugality as stinginess
- ❑ An impulsive shopper
- ❑ A big spender
- ❑ Not good with numbers
- ❑ Someone who hates balancing a checkbook
- ❑ A person who enjoys giving money away
- ❑ Rich enough to be sloppy about money and get away with it
- ❑ Afraid of being seen as a failure

- ❑ Afraid of being seen as greedy
- ❑ Afraid of not providing for my children well enough

8. If you have children, do you feel comfortable discussing money in front of them? Why or why not?

____

____

____

____

Now discuss your responses to questions 4 through 8 with your group, sharing as much as you feel comfortable sharing. What have you learned about yourself?

Why Are You Here?

To stand against the pressure to buy and consume in our culture is as hard as trying to stand still in an ocean with hurricane tides. For one individual or couple to do it alone is nearly impossible. We need each other. That is the purpose of this study guide and its three companion guides: to give you an opportunity to stand together with one or more people.

"If one falls down, his friend can help him up. But pity the man who falls and has no one to help him up! Though one may be overpowered, two can defend themselves. A cord of three strands is not quickly broken" (Ecclesiastes 4:10, 12).

9. Why did you come to this group? Check the appropriate answer(s).

   - ❑ My spouse dragged me here.
   - ❑ The group voted, and I lost.
   - ❑ I'm tired of struggling to make ends meet; there must be something I don't know.
   - ❑ The subject of money fascinates me.
   - ❑ I wanted something from God to counter all the messages I get from the media about what I should do and be.
   - ❑ Other (Describe your situation.)

____

____

10. What do you hope to get out of this study of biblical attitudes about money?

____

____

____

The Grace Adventure

In the Bible, *grace* refers to two generous gifts God gives us. One is the welcoming forgiveness He offers when we fall far short of His standard for a wise and loving life. The other is the empowering presence of the Holy Spirit within us, the Spirit who can enable us to become people we never dreamed of being. Unless we believe firmly that God extends grace to us with both hands, we likely will find that studying His principles about money will produce little but guilt and rationalization. But if we believe in grace, then these same principles can become doorways to an adventure in living by grace.

11. If your group has more than eight members, divide into groups of three. (Or put the men in one group and the women in another.) Tell your group members one thing this session prompts you to ask God for. Then, in a couple of minutes, either in silence together or aloud, ask God to provide those needs.

During the Week

- This week, be alert for how you handle situations that involve money. Watch for one that is typical of you. Maybe it's when you go bargain hunting at the grocery store. Maybe you'll get your bank statement and put it away without looking at it. Perhaps you'll argue with someone over money, or perhaps you'll buy a gift you feel is extravagant. Afterward, write down what you did, how you felt, and what you wanted to accomplish. Did you feel excited, angry, frustrated, affectionate, determined, or scared? Maybe you were aware of feeling nothing at all. As for your goal, were you trying to make ends meet, please someone else, serve God, or do something nice for yourself?

If it's hard for you to identify your feelings and motives, that's okay. This doesn't come naturally for all of us. But do make note of the situation. You'll be sharing it with your group in session 2.

- Second, read "Seeking God's Kingdom" in session 2 (pages 26–27). Does it make sense? Do you disagree with anything there? What questions does it raise for you? Your group will make more progress if everyone has taken time to read this section.
- Third, copy Matthew 6:24 onto a card or sheet of notepaper. Post it where you will see it often during the week—perhaps on your dashboard, over your desk, or on your refrigerator. Each time you see it, read it and think about what significance it has for you. Take note of how it makes you feel. Are you uncomfortable, convicted, or encouraged?

Session 2

GOD'S AGENDA VERSUS THE WORLD'S AGENDA

1. What thoughts came to you about money this week? How have you been feeling about money?

___

___

___

2. At the end of session 1, you were asked to watch for a situation in which you handled money. Explain the following to your group.

    a. What I was trying to accomplish:

___

___

___

    b. How I felt:

___

___

___

c. What someone could learn about me from observing that situation:

____

____

____

Seeking God's Kingdom

The first part of question 2 above has to do with *goals*, *priorities*, and *values*. For example, Marsha is a single mother with two children. When she buys groceries, her goals are to obtain healthy food her children will agree to eat and to spend no more than $100 per week at the grocery store. When she considers an item, she has to weigh several priorities: staying within her budget, pleasing her children, pleasing her own taste buds, limiting food preparation time, building up her children's health, and so on. When she feels two strong values in conflict—feeding her family the best quality food versus staying within her budget—Marsha may feel internal conflict and frustration. When Marsha feels she is able to meet her most important priorities, she probably will feel content.

Goals, priorities, and values are spiritual issues. God created the earth and human beings with certain goals and values in mind. He has an agenda. The Bible presents God's value system. If we haven't read the Bible, we may have no idea what God's values are.

When we do read about God's values in the Bible, our reactions generally fall somewhere between two extremes: "What a wonderful value; isn't God great!" and "That's terrible! What God wants directly conflicts with what I want!" Nowhere does this conflict arise more noticeably than in the area of money.

However, if we believe that God made our planet, it follows that He owns it and has a right to set the agenda. Furthermore, the biblical writers consistently claim that we will be most satisfied if we live by God's values rather than by values we develop on our own. Most of us find this hard to believe and are reluctant to invest all our stock in God's system; but my experience with God's agenda has been overwhelmingly positive, although often not easy.

So what are God's values? What is His agenda?

After Jesus warned both rich and poor in His audience against worshiping mammon (Matthew 6:24), He urged them not to make survival needs (food, clothing) their top priority, but instead to "*Seek first His* [God's] *kingdom and His righteousness; and all these things shall be added to you*" (Matthew 6:33 NASB).

Jesus said the number one protection against being strangled by wealth or crushed by poverty, the number one safeguard against anxiety about or worship of money, is to seek first God's kingdom and His righteousness.

So what does that mean? Jesus says the smartest thing we can do financially is to make His kingdom and His righteousness our top priority. In order to make sense of this statement, we have to understand what He means by "His kingdom" and "His righteousness."

Already But Not Yet

The Jews of Jesus' day were on the edge of their seats,

waiting for God to replace this age (the time of Satan's rule—the time of sin, sickness, and the success of evil people) with the age to come (the time of God's rule—the time of health, justice/righteousness, and peace). Many of the prophets had spoken of the age to come, which the Messiah would bring.

Jesus came announcing that God's kingdom, or the time of God's rule, had arrived because He, the King, had arrived. He read from the prophet Isaiah's description of the One who would establish God's kingdom.

"*The Spirit of the Lord is on me, because he has anointed me to preach good news to the poor. He has sent me to proclaim freedom for the prisoners and recovery of sight for the blind, to release the oppressed, to proclaim the year of the Lord's favor*" (Luke 4:18–19).

Jesus acted out what He proclaimed: He healed the sick, raised the dead, and rebuked the corrupt temple authorities. He empowered and sent His followers to do the same.

"*When Jesus had called the Twelve together, he gave them power and authority to drive out all demons and to cure diseases, and he sent them out to preach the kingdom of God and to heal the sick*" (Luke 9:1–2).

"*After this the Lord appointed seventy-two others and sent them two by two ahead of him to every town and place where he was about to go. He told them, '. . . When you enter a town . . . heal the sick who are there and tell them, "The kingdom of God is near you"*'" (Luke 10:1–2, 8–9).

"The kingdom of God" was a Jewish term for the realm where God ruled with justice (or righteousness) and with what we might call "wholeness." The Greek word *soteria* could be translated as "salvation" or "healing." The

Hebrew word *shalom* could be translated as "peace," "prosperity," "well-being," or "wholeness." The citizens of the kingdom would be whole in body, mind, and spirit; their relationships with each other and God would be whole, and even death would be forgotten.

"*On this mountain he will destroy the shroud that enfolds all peoples, the sheet that covers all nations; he will swallow up death forever. The Sovereign Lord will wipe away the tears from all faces; he will remove the disgrace of his people from all the earth*" (Isaiah 25:7–8).

In His teaching about the kingdom, Jesus envisioned a community where the haves and the have-nots viewed each other as part of one family, one kingdom under one King, all pulling together to care for one another. The materially rich would help the materially poor, the physically well would help heal the physically sick, and the spiritually rich would serve the spiritually impoverished.

The community's mission was a practical kind of love that met the physical and spiritual needs of both insiders and outsiders. The kingdom's two laws were, "'*Love the Lord your God with all your heart and with all your soul and with all your strength and with all your mind*'; *and*, '*Love your neighbor as yourself*'" (Luke 10:27).

Jesus' death temporarily stunned His followers, but His resurrection restored their faith. They were convinced that at any moment He would bring the final fulfillment of His kingdom: overthrow the Romans, stamp out death permanently, and reign over the earth. But after forty days, Jesus left. It didn't take long for His followers to realize that Jesus had been preparing them to live *between* the beginning of the end of this age and the final arrival of the next age.

God's kingdom was *already* but *not yet*. God had begun to rule within each believer but not yet over all the earth. Death was already conquered, yet believers would still die for a while longer. We are *already* free from the penalty for sin, but we are *not yet* free from all temptation and compulsion.

So what? What does this have to do with us and our money? We are citizens of Christ's kingdom and agents of His government, in a world that is still at war against Him. God calls us to use whatever resources we've been given to further the agenda of His government, to spread the values of His rule.

These values are righteousness (justice, ethical living), peace, the news that Jesus is the King, the offer of forgiveness and salvation, wholeness in relationships, neighbors loving neighbors, and so on. We are here to subvert the existing spiritual government wherever we find it.

So if the existing spiritual government says, "You are what you own" and "Shop till you drop," we will resist it. We will band together to build a community where people belong not because they own the right car or the right basketball shoes but because the King has invited them. We will seek to earn our living doing things the King wants done, and we will spend our income on things the King values.

How does this look in practice? Consider Mark, who owns a small film and television production company. His business started twenty years ago with Mark, his wife, a camera, and a roll of film. Today Mark has a dozen employees and hires a hundred or more freelance crew members during any given year. Half of Mark's work is television commercials; the other half consists of values-based youth programming, fund-raising films for missions organizations, and other ministry-related work.

Mark turns down lottery commercials and any advertising that uses sex to sell products. Every Monday morning, his full-time staff and any freelancers who care to attend gather in the conference room for "staff meeting." Staff meeting involves reading a passage from the Bible and talking about how it applies to the lives of the gathered group.

Someone might talk about getting depressed on the weekend and wanting to go back to bingeing on food. Another might talk of sexual temptation or the struggle to manage his or her temper. Another might report a breakthrough conversation with his or her mother. Non-Christian freelancers attend week after week, enthralled by what they see.

Mark and his team do first-class creative work; they are artists serving the ultimate Artist. As an outpost of God's kingdom, their values reflect kingdom values: making enough money to feed their families; creating beauty; teaching truth; loving their neighbors; attracting outsiders to the King.

In years past, Mark's money questions concerned survival: "Should I take that less-than-tasteful commercial job in order to make ends meet?" Now they concern surplus: "Should I buy as much car as I can afford, or is some of that money needed elsewhere?"

All of us face these kinds of questions about money every day. The answers are often difficult, but a crucial first step is understanding that they concern goals, values, and priorities. What does it mean to seek the kingdom first in this situation? What does the King value most in this case? If I can't have everything, what will be my priorities?

3. How do you respond to the story of Mark the filmmaker? Check one.

   - ❑ He has a unique situation, out of reach of most people.
   - ❑ I could do that.
   - ❑ How long did it take to figure all that out?
   - ❑ I don't get this kingdom stuff.
   - ❑ Other (Give your response.)

____

____

____

4. The members of Mark's team make decisions together about how their company will further the kingdom. They also support each other in making personal financial decisions that fit kingdom values. How would having friends like this make it easier to put God's kingdom first?

____

____

____

____

5. Consider the items that are high on God's kingdom agenda. Discuss some ways in which an individual, family, or group of believers could pursue the following priorities.

   Feeding one's family (1 Timothy 5:8)

   Healing the sick (Luke 9:2)

   Freeing the oppressed (Luke 4:18)

Caring for the needy (James 1:27)

Loving neighbors (Luke 10:27)

Inviting people to know the King (Luke 10:9)

6. Suppose you were thinking of buying a new car. How would you go about evaluating whether buying

a new car fit God's agenda for you? What questions would you ask?

7. Take a couple of minutes of silence and write at least one decision about financial priorities you are facing. It may have to do with something you are planning to buy, what line of work you want to be in, an investment, or a gift. Afterward, you may choose whether to tell the group your decision.

The Grace Adventure

8. Divide into groups of three. Spend at least five minutes praying together, silently or aloud. Give each person time to speak his or her mind to God about:
   - something puzzling from this session

- needing wisdom for a financial decision
- gratitude for being part of God's kingdom
- anything else this session prompted you to say

During the Week

- Copy Matthew 6:33 onto a card, and post it near your Matthew 6:24 card. See if you can memorize Matthew 6:33 this week.
- Be alert for a time this week when you have to make a decision, large or small, about money. When the situation occurs, pause and ask yourself, "How does this fit into the priorities of God's kingdom?" Ask God also.
- If you find yourself struggling with this question and have some extra time, start your own quest to understand God's priorities. Begin reading through Matthew's or Luke's Gospel, looking for what Jesus says is important and what He treats as important. What are Jesus' priorities? What does He value? (People, for instance.) Make a list. How important are people compared to other things? Are some people more important than others? It might take you a few months to get through one of the Gospels like this, but it will be time well spent.
- Set aside time to read through session 3 before your next meeting.

Session 3

TRUST VERSUS FEAR

1. What have you been thinking and feeling about money this week?

____

____

____

Birds and Flowers

We've looked at Matthew 6:24, where Jesus warns against worshiping money, and at Matthew 6:33, where He tells us to make building God's kingdom our top priority. Between those verses, Jesus addresses one of the main temptations to take our eyes off the kingdom and focus them on money: worry.

"No one can serve two masters. Either he will hate the one and love the other, or he will be devoted to the one and despise the other. You cannot serve both God and Money.

Therefore I tell you, **do not worry** *about your life, what you will eat or drink; or about your body, what you will wear. Is not life more important than food, and the body more important than clothes? Look at the birds of the air; they do not sow or reap or store away in barns, and yet your heavenly Father feeds them. Are you not much more valuable than they? Who of you by worrying can add a single hour to his life?*

"And **why do you worry** *about clothes? See how the lilies of the field grow. They do not labor or spin. Yet I tell you that not even Solomon in all his splendor was dressed like one of these. If that is how God clothes the grass of the field, which is here today and tomorrow is thrown into the fire, will he not much more clothe you, O you of little faith?*

"So **do not worry,** *saying, 'What shall we eat?' or 'What shall we drink?' or 'What shall we wear?' For the pagans run after all these things, and your heavenly Father knows that you need them. But seek first his kingdom and his righteousness, and all these things will be given to you as well. Therefore* **do not worry** *about tomorrow, for tomorrow will worry about itself. Each day has enough trouble of its own"* (Matthew 6:24–34, emphasis added).

Jesus was speaking to Third World peasants who owned not more than two, and probably only one, change of clothing. Each day's wages paid for that day's food. There was no option of putting the groceries on the credit card if the paycheck didn't arrive. (At the same time, there was no pressure to buy one's children the right clothes or the latest toys, let alone saving for college.) So in most ways, Jesus' original audience had more reasons to be anxious about making ends meet than we do; yet Jesus repeated, *do not worry*.

2. What reasons does Jesus give in this passage for not worrying about money?

____

____

____

3. How much of a money-worrier are you? Circle one number.

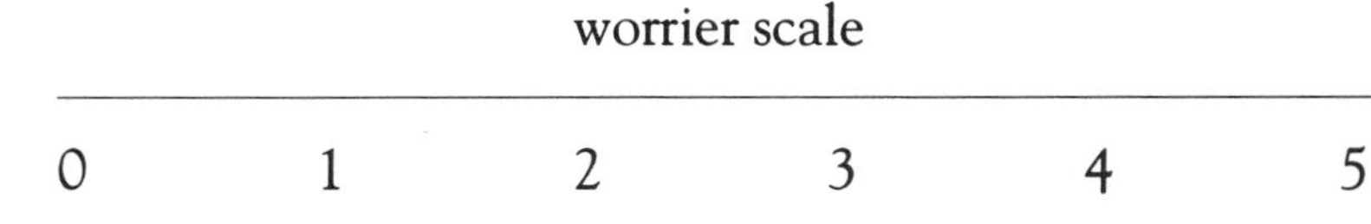

not at all obsessive about worry

4. If you rated yourself at higher than 1 on the worrier scale, which of Jesus' reasons for not worrying do you find less than convincing?

5. Take five minutes on your own to write answers to questions a–c below. You won't have to share your answers if you prefer not to.

   a. If you tend to worry about money, what do the anxious voices in your head say? Write some of the things they say. (For example, "If you go broke, you'll have to go crawling back to your father, and what will he think of you then?" Or, "We'll end up on the street with no where to go and nothing to eat.")

b. Whose voice do you hear saying those things? Is it your own? A family member's? The devil's?

c. What do you think God would say to this voice?

d. Tell the group anything you learned from this exercise that you feel comfortable sharing.

6. Maybe you're not a worrier, but your spouse or one of your parents is a worrier. How does that person's worry affect you?

____

____

____

I know one person who insists that worry works because nothing she has ever seriously worried about has happened. However, most of us find that worry is much less useful. It takes energy away from planning and carrying out courageous action that might improve our financial situations. Worry paralyzes us. Why do we do it, then?

Virginia highly values security. It's very important to her to have a safe environment for raising her children. She feels vulnerable to the ravages of the world unless their food, shelter, and clothing are 100 percent guaranteed. Unpaid bills make her feel insecure, unprotected. She knows that if she, as a woman, loses everything and ends up on the street, she will find many reasons to be frightened there.

Virginia's challenge, then, is to take her deeply ingrained longing for security to God. Can He be trusted to provide for His daughter as He provides for the birds? Or will He abandon her at a critical moment? A woman like Virginia who struggles with worry may need to wrestle with God over Matthew 6:24–34, as well as the following.

"Do not be anxious about anything, but in everything, by prayer and petition, with thanksgiving, present your

requests to God. And the peace of God, which transcends all understanding, will guard your hearts and your minds in Christ Jesus" (Philippians 4:6–7).

Shelly has no children and makes a decent salary, so she doesn't have to worry about her family starving. But as a single woman, Shelly knows she's on her own, and security remains a top priority. She buys a new car every five years and keeps it carefully maintained; she hates to risk it breaking down on the highway at night.

Shelly spends a bit more than she can really afford on an apartment with a security system even though she's in a very low crime area. She has a hard time budgeting money to give to her church because saving for her retirement feels more important. Shelly thinks of herself as frugal—certainly not stingy. But deep down, she believes she can afford to invest in God's kingdom only *after* her security needs are taken care of.

Unlike Shelly's and Virginia's concerns for security, Dave's worries stem from fear of failure. He dreads letting his family down and letting his dad see him as inadequate. The ten-year-old inside Dave still cringes at his father's stinging words when he brought home a D in science, and, even though his dad hasn't criticized him in years, Dave still flinches every month when the credit card bill arrives.

Dave may need to humble himself before God, admit his limitations, and trust God to supply what he lacks. At the same time, he needs to confess his tendency to equate his Heavenly Father with his critical earthly father. Dave must accept the fact that God has put within him the power of the Holy Spirit to equip him with self-confidence and courage.

Dave needs to read what God said to Joshua: "*Be strong and courageous. Do not be terrified; do not be discouraged, for the Lord your God will be with you wherever you go*" (Joshua 1:9). Dave needs to believe that God is offering the same to him that He offered to Joshua.

God calls all of us to humble ourselves, trust in Him, and take courageous action in the face of financial worries.

7. Can you identify with Virginia, Shelly, or Dave in any ways? If so, how? If not, how are you different?

____

____

____

8. Why do you suppose it's so hard for many of us to trust God with our finances?

____

____

____

____

9. When you think about humbly trusting and courageously acting, how do you feel? Do those seem like stances you are capable of taking with regard to your finances? Why or why not?

10. How can the group pray for you this week?

The Grace Adventure

11. Ask for volunteers to pray for each of the requests from question 10. Allow about five minutes for prayer.

During the Week

- Copy either Philippians 4:6–7 or Joshua 1:9 onto a card. Post it next to Matthew 6:24 and 6:33. As you notice these verses during the week, ask, "What common theme do I see emerging here?"
- Listen for the expressions of worry this week. Listen for the critical voices that tempt you to be anxious instead of courageous and for the nervous voices that tempt you to fear instead of trusting God. When they speak, hear them out. If possible, write what they say. Ask them: "Really? Tell me

more. Why is that?" You may find them losing power just because you've shined the clear light of day on them. Quote the verses from Matthew or Philippians or Joshua to them and see what they say. Talk to God about what the voices say, and ask Him to help you sort truth from falsehood.

- Read session 4 before your next meeting.

Session 4

CONTENTMENT VERSUS GREED

1. What have you been thinking and feeling about money this week?

____

____

2. Have you noticed any voices of anxiety about money since session 3? What have you learned since beginning to pay attention to those voices?

____

____

How Much Is Enough?

The apostle Paul was raised in a fairly affluent family for his time. They were able to pay for his education with one of the foremost rabbis in Jerusalem. Nevertheless, after he encountered Christ, Paul chose to spend the last two or three decades of his life in very uncertain financial circumstances.

For months at a time he walked across what is now Turkey, a region of steep hills, strong sun and stronger storms, scarce water, abundant bandits, rare inns, and rarer towns. Sometimes Paul found an affluent host who offered a solid dinner and a soft bed. More often, Paul camped by the roadside.

Eventually he spent a few years in some prisons whose living conditions compared to what one might enjoy in Iraq today. From one of those jail cells, Paul wrote to his friends in Philippi, thanking them for a financial gift.

In that letter he wrote, "*I have learned to be content whatever the circumstances. I know what it is to be in need, and I know what it is to have plenty. I have learned the secret of being content in any and every situation, whether well fed or hungry, whether living in plenty or in want. I can do everything through him who gives me strength*" (Philippians 4:11–13).

Paul had learned something rare: the ability to live with equal contentment in a tenement or in a mansion.

Some of us imagine that contentment is synonymous with a big bank balance: *If* we have X amount of money, *then* we will be content. But our society is the wealthiest that has ever existed on earth, and many of its wealthiest members live on alcohol and tranquilizers so, clearly, contentment does not depend on income.

Nor is contentment simply being satisfied with where you are. There's nothing especially godly about stagnation and lack of goals. Instead, *contentment is knowing God's plan for your life, having the conviction to live it, and believing that God's peace is bigger than the world's problems.*

Still, being discontented with their standard of living plagues many people. In some ways it was easier to be content in Paul's day, when 98 percent of the population lived well below what we consider the poverty line.

If all of our neighbors drove old cars; lived in cramped apartments; and owned six outfits, two pairs of shoes, and fewer than a dozen CDs; we would find it easier to be content with the same. On the other hand, it's very hard to be content with less than what your neighbors own, especially if they treat you like you don't belong to their social class.

As humans, it's normal for us to want to feel that we belong to our community. Unfortunately, our society measures human worth by possessions. Advertising blares its propaganda: "You need more. If you don't have this, you'll be left out. If you buy this, people will desire you; if you buy that, they'll respect you." In our culture, greed is a virtue. Only in its most extreme form is it ever considered sinful.

A God's Eye View

In God's kingdom, however, greed is much more serious. "*Do you not know that the wicked will not inherit the kingdom of God? Do not be deceived: Neither the sexually immoral nor idolaters nor adulterers nor male prostitutes nor homosexual offenders nor thieves* **nor the greedy** *nor drunkards nor slanderers nor swindlers will inherit the kingdom of God*" (1 Corinthians 6:9–10, emphasis added).

Are you surprised that greed is up there with adultery and male prostitution as one of the things we should never dream of doing? Don't be. Paul also wrote, "*But now I am writing you that you must not associate with anyone who calls himself a brother but is sexually immoral or* **greedy**, *an idolater or a slanderer, a drunkard or a swindler. With such a man do not even eat*" (1 Corinthians 5:11, emphasis added).

To Paul, it was so inconceivable that people could call

themselves Christians and be greedy, he wouldn't have anything to do with such people.

Thankfully, God is merciful. He understands the pressure we are under to "belong" to our culture, and He offers forgiveness and the power to change. He invites us to join a different culture with a different set of values and different rules for belonging: the kingdom of God.

Paul continues, "*And that* [adulterers, male prostitutes, and greedy people] *is what some of you* were. *But you were washed, you were sanctified, you were justified in the name of the Lord Jesus Christ and by the Spirit of our God*" (1 Corinthians 6:11).

Remember Mark's filmmaking team from session 2? The question of greed comes up regularly in their shop. It's not surprising that people in the TV commercial business watch television and are affected by commercials.

They also appreciate technological gadgets: the latest cameras, recording equipment, and stereo systems. If you care about set design, you also probably care about the interior decoration of your home and office. And of course you need to look your best when courting potential clients; you wouldn't want to wear a cheap suit or drive a cheap car.

Nobody on Mark's team finds these decisions easy. Their strategy is to talk about financial decisions together, admit their tendency toward greed, and wrestle over kingdom values. They reinforce in each other a biblical assessment of what they need versus what they merely want. It's like keeping *down* with the Joneses.

They also have outside help. They film regularly in American ghettos and in the Third World. Nothing clarifies needs and wants like spending time in a housing project.

Finally, they pray for what they want. Praying for what we want is different from complaining to God about what we don't have. Asking has a way of sorting out wants that are valid from wants that are greedy. Asking says we believe God is good.

"Which of you, if his son asks for bread, will give him a stone? Or if he asks for a fish, will give him a snake? If you, then, though you are evil, know how to give good gifts to your children, how much more will your Father in heaven give good gifts to those who ask him!" (Matthew 7:9–11).

Like Paul, Mark's team wants to learn to move freely between wealth and poverty and to find contentment in doing God's will, not in what they own.

Write answers to questions 3 through 5 on your own.

3. How often do you see an advertisement and think, "I want that." Check one.

- ❑ Once a month
- ❑ Once a week
- ❑ Several times a week
- ❑ More than seven times a week

4. How often do you see someone's home, car, outfit, or technological gadget and wish for what they have? Check one.

- ❑ Once a year

- ❑ Several times a year
- ❑ Once a month
- ❑ Several times a month
- ❑ Once a week
- ❑ More than once a week

5. Based on your answers to questions 3 and 4, would you say greed is a problem for you? Why?

6. Have you recently yielded to greed? If so, explain.

7. How does having children make it harder for families to be content with less than others have?

8. How does it feel to think of yourself as struggling with greed? Is that uncomfortable? Why?

9. How would your level of contentment be affected if your circle of close friends were all committed to resisting greed?

10. If this group could support you in one area of contentment versus greed, what would that be?

The Grace Adventure

Paul says we "*were justified in the name of the Lord Jesus Christ and by the Spirit of our God.*" That means we are welcomed into God's kingdom because of Christ's work, despite our ongoing struggles with greed and discontent. God's Spirit lives in us to make contentment possible.

11. Use question 10 as a basis for prayer; pray for each other in your areas of struggle. Ask God to show you the difference between what you *need* and what you *want*. Ask Him to show you which of your wants are consistent with what He wants for you and which are not.

During the Week

- Review your posted verses this week: Matthew 6:24 and 6:33, Philippians 4:6–7, or Joshua 1:9. How do these verses encourage contentment and undermine greed?
- Watch one half hour of television and look for the messages that encourage greed. (You might do this with someone else in your group.) Notice the advertising messages, of course, but also pay attention to the lifestyles of the people in the program. Does what you see encourage you to value God's kingdom or to buy more things?
- Read session 5 before your next meeting.

Session 5

HUMILITY VERSUS PRIDE

1. a. Did you look for greed messages on television this week? What did you observe?

___

___

___

   b. How did what you saw affect you personally? For instance, did you find yourself drawn into wanting what you saw on television, or did the greed messages turn you off?

___

___

___

Pride, Shame, and Humility

In the film *Beaches*, Bette Midler says to someone she has recently met, "But enough about me. Let's talk about you. What do *you* think—about me?"

Most of us don't flaunt our self-centeredness that openly, but secretly we believe the world revolves around us. Pride is the core issue for the business executive who thinks he needs a $2 million airplane so he won't have to wait in airport lines. It's also an issue for the urban teenager who sells drugs in order to buy the right jacket. Maybe a few of us lust for the best food, clothes, and electronics out of pure sensual pleasure, but for most of us greed is closely linked to status. And status is about pride. What does "keeping up with the Joneses" mean if it doesn't mean proving we're as successful as they are?

We care enormously about what other people think of us. It's as if our very lives depend upon it. Thirteen-year-old Teri shoplifts panty hose from a department store because she is the only girl in her class who can't afford to buy them. For the lack of this small status symbol, Teri is treated as an outcast. It makes her feel ashamed. Who can fail to feel compassion for her?

Teri's shame and humiliation are the result of trusting the wrong source for a sense of worth. Teri needs a family and friends who will treat her as if her worth has nothing to do with what she owns. The more Teri understands that her worth comes from God's love for her, the more she will relax and feel humility not humiliation.

Humble people don't waste time thinking, "I'm better than she is," or, "I'm nobody." Humble people are comfortable with themselves and free to care for others; they don't need to play status games.

Many people confuse shame (the belief that one is inferior or worthless) with humility. On the contrary, shame and pride are two sides of the same coin: both reflect an obsessive concern with whether someone is valuable in other people's eyes. Likewise, many people confuse self-confidence with pride. However, it's possible to be confident in one's own worth and even one's own skills and yet be humble.

Jesus was supremely confident in His worth and His abilities. The Pharisees did everything they could to shame Him, but He had no ego at stake and no self-doubt, so He never fell for their tricks. Money has very little allure for anyone who has a settled confidence and humility.

pride humility

<———————————————————————>

shame self-confidence

Sure Signs

One sure sign of pride is thinking we're making it on our own. Moses warned the Israelites, "*Be careful that you do not forget the Lord your God, failing to observe his commands, his laws and his decrees that I am giving you this day. Otherwise, when you eat and are satisfied, when you build fine houses and settle down, and when your herds and flocks grow large and your silver and gold increase and all you have is multiplied,* **then your heart will become proud and you will forget the Lord your God,** *who brought you out of Egypt, out of the land of slavery.*

"*You may say to yourself, 'My power and the strength of my hands have produced this wealth for me.' But remember the Lord your God, for it is he who gives you the ability to produce wealth, and so confirms his covenant, which he swore to your forefathers, as it is today*" (Deuteronomy 8:11–14, 17–18, emphasis added).

If we are financially successful, we have God to thank for giving us abilities, education, health, and opportunity in the wealthiest nation on earth.

If you have enough money that worry is not a problem for you, you can bet that pride is hovering somewhere nearby, waiting to swallow you whole. And if you do worry, ask yourself how much of your worry relates to pride. "What would our friends think if they knew we couldn't really afford this?" "What if I lose my job and have to sell the house? People will think I'm a loser." "Do I dress well enough to fit in?"

Another sure sign of pride is treating other people according to how much money they make. Once I was working against a deadline on some important material, and a widow I had been counseling phoned me. I was a little irritated because she had been in to see me several times, with relatively trivial problems. She asked if she could come in right away because she had a crisis in her budget: her checking account didn't balance. I explained that I really didn't have any time available and suggested another counselor we had trained.

A short time later I received a call from a businessman who wanted to bring by a celebrity who was in town working on a movie. I knew it was a rare opportunity, and I said yes to him.

As soon as I hung up the phone the words of James rang in my ears. "*But if you show favoritism, you sin and are convicted by the law as lawbreakers*" (James 2:9). I had to call the businessman back and tell him I could not meet with them until later; then I called my counselee back and asked her forgiveness.

Jesus set the ultimate example of humility. He who was God, who owned everything, did not hesitate to come to earth to associate with us lowly humans. If we judge others by their possessions or their incomes, if we measure human worth in dollars, then we can hardly blame children for selling drugs or stealing in order to prove their worth.

We may not notice the signs of pride in ourselves, but others certainly do. However, if they know we're too proud to take constructive criticism, they won't tell us. Spouses are especially positioned to spot our pride and if we're wise, we'll make it safe for them to speak and we'll listen to what they say. We should also cultivate friends who will tell us the truth about ourselves.

2. How might pride be a factor in each of the following situations?

   The decision to buy a new car

   ___

   ___

   ___

   The choice of schools for your children

   ___

   ___

   ___

   The choice of where to live

   ___

   ___

Your choice of friends

3. What's the difference between shame and humility?

4. What's the difference between self-confidence and pride?

5. Why is it so hard to keep in mind that our abilities to succeed at work and make money come from God?

6. Why is it hard not to measure ourselves and others in dollar value?

7. It's awkward to confess your pride to someone else without sounding either falsely humble or just plain boastful: "I did this incredibly brilliant thing at work, and of course everybody was so impressed, and I confess I felt a bit proud. . . ." "No, no, it was nothing really. All the glory goes to God. . . ."

   Take a minute on your own to write about a recent time when you let pride affect a buying decision or a judgment about a person.

8. How would cultivating humility make it easier not to slip into greed and overspending?

____

____

____

____

9. How can a group of Christian friends encourage each other to be humble, as opposed to proud or ashamed of their financial status?

____

____

____

The Grace Adventure

"God opposes the proud but gives grace to the humble" (James 4:6). We close the door to God when we are proud, because the proud person says, "I don't need God's forgiveness or His power to change. I'm just fine as I am. I can handle it." But the smallest gesture of humility, such as confessing proud attitudes, opens that door so God can provide forgiveness and grace.

10. Take a few minutes of silence in which to confess your pride to God. Tell Him specifically about any financial decisions you've made, or are considering,

that pride has influenced. If you've been treating people differently according to their incomes, how they look, or what they do for a living, tell God about that. Ask Him to show you if you need to ask anyone's forgiveness.

During the Week

- Post James 4:6 with the rest of your key verses from this study.
- If you're married, ask your spouse what signs of pride or arrogance he or she sees in you. If you're not married, ask a friend who knows you well. Pray ahead of time for a humble receptiveness to what you hear.
- Read session 6 before your next meeting.

Session 6

GRATITUDE VERSUS RESENTMENT

A New Perspective

Doug could never remember a time as a child when his parents weren't struggling to make ends meet. Doug was the first in his family to go to college, so when a respected private school offered him partial financial aid, Doug didn't flinch at borrowing to pay for the rest of his expenses.

After college Doug went on to earn a master's degree, which required more loans. Doug decided he wanted to teach, and even though he enjoyed his work, paying off student loans stretched his budget. He eventually married, and again, although he loved his family, by the time his second son was six or seven years old, Doug was getting depressed.

He loved art and foreign films, but he was beginning to realize he might never see Paris or India. He couldn't even afford to take his kids to Disneyland, never mind Europe. His wife talked about how her friend's husband still took her on romantic dates after all these years, and Doug said nothing. He didn't want to admit, even to himself, how badly he felt that he couldn't afford to take his wife out. Doug felt he had spent his whole life struggling to catch up financially with everybody else, and he was tired of it. He would never catch up.

He finally went to see a financial counselor from church, thinking maybe there was something wrong with the way he was managing his money. But after looking over his expenses and discussing some options, the counselor said something that stopped Doug cold: "I wonder if it would help if you spent less time thinking about what you don't have and more time thanking God for what you do have?"

It seemed so simple. Doug thought back to when he had been grateful for the chance to go to college—before he started resenting having to repay his student loans. He made a list of things God had done for him: given him a job he liked (okay, so it would never make him a millionaire); slowly but surely enabled him to reduce his debts (he might actually be debt-free in a couple of years); given him a great wife and two terrific sons (expensive but worth it). So maybe he would never own a house or get to Europe. Maybe seeing heaven someday would make up for not seeing the Sistine Chapel.

Gratitude can transform our attitudes toward our lives and finances. It's a sign that we're growing in the other positive attitudes we've been discussing: trust, contentment, and humility. It's also an antidote to the negative attitudes: worry, greed, and pride.

"Do not be anxious about anything, but in everything, by prayer and petition, **with thanksgiving**, *present your requests to God. And the peace of God, which transcends all understanding, will guard your hearts and your minds in Christ Jesus"* (Philippians 4:6–7, emphasis added).

It's hard to *make* ourselves stop worrying, but we can decide to ask God for what we want, thank Him for what

He's already given, and thank Him for being the kind of good Father who gives good gifts to His children. Cultivating gratitude reminds us that God is good and, therefore, we don't need to worry. The more grateful we are for what we do have, the harder it becomes to lust for what we don't have or to envy others for having it.

Imagine if, instead of worrying about losing her financial security, Virginia (session 3) thanked God for providing food, shelter, and clothing for her and her children? Imagine if Shelly started thanking God for being her protector. Would she feel safe enough to be more generous with her money? If Dave could thank God for being a good Father and for making him a man, would he have more courage to face his financial pressures squarely?

Gratitude displaces pride equally well. Instead of patting ourselves on the back for our financial successes, we remember gratefully that even our abilities come from God.

"*You may say to yourself, 'My power and the strength of my hands have produced this wealth for me.'* **But remember the Lord your God**, *for it is he who gives you the ability to produce wealth, and so confirms his covenant, which he swore to your forefathers, as it is today*" (Deuteronomy 8:17–18, emphasis added).

A Time to Celebrate

At the end of each fiscal year, Mark the filmmaker and his team take time to thank God for making their company prosper during that year. In boom years they spend a little money celebrating, just as the Israelites set aside money each year to celebrate the Feasts of Firstfruits and Tabernacles at the beginning and end of the harvest season (Deuteronomy 26:1–15). Even in lean years Dave and his team have been able to thank God for keeping them in business.

Recently, one of their clients lost funding at the last minute for a huge project: a full month of work. Preproduction had been done; freelancers had been hired. Now a month of expected income had evaporated. In years past, Mark would have felt paralyzed. Now he and his team looked for an opportunity in the crisis: Was there something they had been wanting to do but had been too busy to pursue? They ended up spending the month brainstorming and pursuing leads, several of which eventually bore fruit. The disaster took a bite out of that year's profits, but the team was still able to celebrate God at work.

"When you have entered the land the Lord your God is giving you as an inheritance and have taken possession of it and settled in it, take some of the firstfruits of all that you produce from the soil of the land the Lord your God is giving you and put them in a basket. Then go to the place the Lord your God will choose as a dwelling for his Name and say to the priest in office at the time, 'I declare today to the Lord your God that I have come to the land the Lord swore to our forefathers to give us.'

"The priest shall take the basket from your hands and set it down in front of the altar of the Lord your God. Then you shall declare before the Lord your God: 'My father was a wandering Aramean, and he went down into Egypt with a few people and lived there and became a great nation, powerful and numerous. But the Egyptians mistreated us and made us suffer, putting us to hard labor. Then we cried out to the

Lord, the God of our fathers, and the Lord heard our voice and saw our misery, toil and oppression.

"So the Lord brought us out of Egypt with a mighty hand and an outstretched arm, with great terror and with miraculous signs and wonders. He brought us to this place and gave us this land, a land flowing with milk and honey; and now I bring the firstfruits of the soil that you, O Lord, have given me.'

"Place the basket before the Lord your God and bow down before him. And you and the Levites and the aliens among you shall **rejoice in all the good things the Lord your God has given to you and your household"** (Deuteronomy 26:1–11, emphasis added).

1. From the above Scripture, what "good things" did the Israelites thank God for each year?

___

___

___

___

2. What are some similar good things that Christians can thank God for?

___

___

___

___

3. Why do you think gratitude affected Doug so strongly?

4. Can you identify with Doug in any ways? If so, how?

5. How is gratitude an antidote to

   worry?

   greed?

pride?

6. What do you think about Mark's custom of celebrating the end of his business fiscal year?

7. When are some appropriate occasions for families to celebrate how well God provides for them?

When going through hard times, it can be terribly hard to cultivate gratitude. Pretending to be grateful when we're not isn't spiritual—just hypocritical. On the other hand, sincerely looking for reasons to be grateful, even if we have to thank God with empty hands, can help strengthen us enough to keep going.

"Though the fig tree does not bud and there are no grapes

on the vines, though the olive crop fails and the fields produce no food, though there are no sheep in the pen and no cattle in the stalls, yet I will rejoice in the Lord, I will be joyful in God my Savior. The Sovereign Lord is my strength; he makes my feet like the feet of a deer, he enables me to go on the heights" (Habakkuk 3:17–19).

8. How easy is it for you to be genuinely grateful to God right now? Explain.

____

____

____

9. As a group, how can you celebrate God's financial provision for each of you?

____

____

____

The Grace Adventure

Perhaps some in your group feel like celebrating; things are going well, and they feel like thanking God. Perhaps some in your group are struggling, and gratitude has to be a choice for them, as it was for the prophet Habakkuk in the passage above. Either way, the grace of God meets each person where he or she is.

10. Take five or ten minutes for the group to thank God for what He has given to each of you. You could form a circle and sing some songs of thanksgiving or pray aloud. You could have someone read a psalm of thanks, such as Psalm 107; or perhaps the passage from Habakkuk might feel more appropriate. Do whatever seems like a genuine expression of your gratitude to God.

During the Week

- Post the verse *"Be joyful always; pray continually; give thanks in all circumstances, for this is God's will for you in Christ Jesus"* (1 Thessalonians 5:16–18).
- Take half an hour to list things for which you are grateful to God.
- Read session 7.

Session 7

JUSTICE VERSUS DECEIT

1. What is one thing you were able to thank God for this week?

____

____

Neighbors

When we think of justice, most of us picture a court of law in which two lawyers battle to convince a judge or jury of their client's position in the case. We consider it foolish, or even criminal, for the lawyers, judge, or jury to have any personal relationships with each other, the defendant, or the plaintiff. That is called a "conflict of interest."

In the Bible, however, the terms *justice* and *righteousness* relate to personal relationships. God expresses righteousness by establishing relationships with individuals, especially the family of Abraham. People are called "just" or "righteous" when they live up to the obligations of their relationships with God and with each other. God gives a body of law to define the basic principles of just dealings between people; and the law assumes that those people are not merely strangers, but they are neighbors who have personal ties.

"Do not pervert justice; do not show partiality to the poor or favoritism to the great, but judge your neighbor fairly. Do

not hate your brother in your heart. Rebuke your neighbor frankly so you will not share in his guilt. Do not seek revenge or bear a grudge against one of your people, but love your neighbor as yourself" (Leviticus 19:15,17–18).

God declared Himself the defender of justice, of right dealings between neighbors, whether the matter concerned fair weights and measures in buying and selling (Deuteronomy 25:13–15) or the protection of the poor.

"*For the Lord your God is God of gods and Lord of lords, the great God, mighty and awesome, who shows no partiality and accepts no bribes. He defends the cause of the fatherless and the widow, and loves the alien, giving him food and clothing*" (Deuteronomy 10:17–18).

The Israelites assumed that a neighbor was someone of their nationality, but even from the first statement of the law, God wanted His people to recognize the aliens or strangers among them as their neighbors. Jesus underscored this point in His parable of the Good Samaritan (Luke 10:25–37). In the kingdom of God there are no strangers, only neighbors and family members to whom we owe justice as a matter of family loyalty and concern.

So when we think of justice in financial matters, we need to keep this idea of personal relationship in mind. Exploiting a contract loophole is unjust, not because it's illegal (it may be perfectly legal, technically), but because it violates a personal relationship. In our day, when we rarely know our neighbors personally, let alone the people with whom we do business or the people who benefit from government programs a thousand miles away, it's easy to stop thinking of them as neighbors. When we exaggerate a product's benefits, steal another person's client, cheat on taxes, or pad an expense report, we may forget we are harming a neighbor, someone to whom we have personal ties.

Mark and Macon

It seems to Mark that he faces a decision about justice or honesty at least six times a day. For instance, TV commercials are contracted through itemized bids; Mark's producer compiles a list of costs that will go into making the commercial—everything from the set designer's daily fee to the cost of film to the wear and tear on the editing equipment. When a client is likely to agree, it's always tempting to pad a bid to protect the company from unforeseen expenses.

Then, of course, there's the perennial question of what to pay each employee and what company benefits to offer. Again, can Mark claim his cable TV subscription as a business expense on his taxes because he needs to watch a certain amount of television in order to keep up on the latest production techniques? And as if all that weren't enough, Mark can't avoid questions about justice in the wider society in which he lives.

Last year Mark was filming in an urban housing project. He met nineteen-year-old Macon, who was considering the claims of Christ but who had a problem. Macon earned his living selling drugs. Macon wanted to be a Christian, but if he gave up selling drugs, he had no training or references with which to get an alternate job. Furthermore, if by some miracle he did get another job, he couldn't continue to live in his neighborhood, because if he quit dealing he would put himself outside the system that protected his car from being stolen and himself from being a target of violence. Macon and his possessions were safe on the streets because protection (the inner-city version of health care) was one of the fringe benefits offered by the organization he worked for.

So Macon wondered if Mark thought it would be okay with God if he kept dealing drugs until he could earn his GED. Macon also wondered if Mark could help him get a job. Macon's questions sent Mark to prayer. What would justice look like in Macon's life, and what was Mark's part in it?

Keeping Ourselves Honest

Problems like Macon's may feel overwhelming and paralyzing to us. What can we do for the Macons of the world? Some of us in far easier circumstances feel we can't possibly survive without tipping the scales in our favor. Deep down, we don't believe God owns the world and is committed to caring for us.

I have found that committing myself ahead of time to the disciplines of confession and restitution makes dishonesty much less attractive. If I know ahead of time that if I cheat someone I will have to go to him or her afterward and admit it, the fear of that unpleasant experience deters me. Also, if I know I'm committed to giving back whatever I might have gained through dishonesty, cheating has even less appeal. But the most essential thing I try to keep in mind is that if I cheat someone—even if it seems that I'm cheating an institution like the government or a big corporation that can afford it—I'm really abusing a personal relationship with neighbors, family members, and God (and not necessarily in that order).

When Zacchaeus finally experienced this truth about personal relationships, his life was transformed. Zacchaeus was a chief tax collector for the Romans, and he had made a lot of money squeezing taxes out of his fellow Jews. The Roman tax system makes ours look gracious and compassionate.

Rome hired as chief tax collector in a particular locality the man who promised to deliver the most revenue. Anything the collector made over and above that promised amount was his profit. Chief tax collectors hired thugs whose job was to collect whatever they could by whatever means necessary. Zacchaeus knew he was a despicable person, and he knew he had sold out any relationships he had ever had with his Jewish neighbors.

But when Jesus arrived in Jericho one day, everything changed.

"*A man was there by the name of Zacchaeus; he was a chief tax collector and was wealthy. He wanted to see who Jesus was, but being a short man he could not, because of the crowd. So he ran ahead and climbed a sycamore-fig tree to see him, since Jesus was coming that way.*

"*When Jesus reached the spot, he looked up and said to him, 'Zacchaeus, come down immediately. I must stay at your house today.' So he came down at once and welcomed him gladly.*

"*All the people saw this and began to mutter, 'He has gone to be the guest of a "sinner"'*" (Luke 19:2–7).

Jesus announced in front of the whole town that He wanted to stay with Zacchaeus. This was an offer of neighborliness, of intimate friendship, that Zacchaeus knew he didn't deserve. Zacchaeus was so moved by Jesus' offer that in an instant he decided to turn his back on unjust affluence and make relationships his top priority.

Before an astonished crowd Zacchaeus said, "*Look, Lord! Here and now I give half of my possessions to the poor, and if I have cheated anybody out of anything, I will pay back four times the amount*" (Luke 19: 8).

Imagine viewing as neighbors, with whom you have bonds of relationship, the local tax collector, like Zacchaeus; a drug dealer, like Macon; your boss and the shareholders of your company; your clients and customers; and your family. Suddenly, justice is not a legal contest between competitors; it is an expression of commitment.

2. What do you think of this idea—that treating people justly is an expression of personal relationship and commitment? How is that like or unlike the way you have previously thought of justice?

3. Why do you think Zacchaeus was so eager to go straight and even pay back four times what he had extorted?

4. How do you feel when you read the story of Mark and Macon?

5. What would you say to Macon if he asked you what he asked Mark?

6. What are some issues of justice and honesty that you face

   in your work?

in your personal life?

as a citizen of your city or country?

7. Why do you think it is hard for many people to believe God will care for them if they resolve to be honest in all their dealings?

8. How can friends help each other live justly and honestly?

The Grace Adventure

Out of all the citizens of Jericho, Jesus chose Zacchaeus as his host, even *before* Zacchaeus resolved to renounce his dishonest ways. Jesus makes the first move toward us, reaching out a hand of friendship even when we are still mired in our unjust habits.

Then Jesus' offer of relationship becomes our motivation to treat others with a kind of justice that expresses neighborly commitment. He offers to walk with us through the painful process of admitting our wrongs, making restitution, and changing our practices.

9. Take some time for silent prayer to confess any acts of dishonesty that come to mind. You might plan five or ten minutes for group members to write down what they want to say to God.

During the Week

- Post this verse from the prophet Micah: "*He has showed you, O man, what is good. And what does the Lord require of you? To act justly and to love mercy and to walk humbly with your God*" (Micah 6:8).
- This week watch for opportunities to choose justice over injustice.
- Read session 8.

Session 8

GENEROSITY VERSUS SELFISHNESS

1. Were you aware this week of having to make any decisions regarding justice or honesty? If so, what decision did you face? What was the issue involved?

____

____

____

From Justice to Generosity

Jeff runs the maintenance department for a small Christian college. Everybody knows him and his wife, Carol. Single women in their church and on the college staff especially love Jeff for his willingness to help them with personal needs. If a garbage disposal breaks, something heavy needs to be hauled, or a piece of furniture requires assembly, people call Jeff.

Carol feels torn. On the one hand, she values her husband's skills and his generous nature. On the other hand, when Jeff disappears all Saturday morning to help someone else, Carol clenches her jaw at the thought of her own home projects that sit uncompleted. Then she feels guilty for being selfish. Wouldn't God like for her to be as generous as Jeff? A voice inside her says, "Charity begins at home." Another voice says, "Yes, but does it stop there?"

No doubt Jeff and Carol could spend their whole lives keeping their own home and family going and never have anything left over for others. On the other hand, they could also spend their whole lives doing things for others and never take care of their own needs. Carol figures the right balance lies somewhere in between—but where?

Most of us have felt the tension Carol faces, the question of when and how to be generous. At what point does taking care of ourselves become selfishness? If justice means fulfilling the obligations of our neighbor/family relationships, and if every human being is our neighbor, then justice quickly begins to require enormous generosity. There are far more needs in the world than we can possibly meet. If we've ever given money to a charity, our address is on the mailing list of thirty organizations, all of which could do wonderful things for the kingdom of God with our money.

Some of us feel that even keeping up with our immediate family needs propels us on a relentless treadmill. We feel too tired to be generous. Barraged with demands from all sides, we read Jesus' instructions with bewilderment.

"Give to everyone who asks you, and if anyone takes what belongs to you, do not demand it back. Do to others as you would have them do to you.

"If you love those who love you, what credit is that to you? Even 'sinners' love those who love them. And if you do good to those who are good to you, what credit is that to you? Even 'sinners' do that. And if you lend to those from

whom you expect repayment, what credit is that to you? Even 'sinners' lend to 'sinners,' expecting to be repaid in full. But love your enemies, do good to them, and lend to them without expecting to get anything back. Then your reward will be great, and you will be sons of the Most High, because he is kind to the ungrateful and wicked. Be merciful, just as your Father is merciful" (Luke 6:30–36).

"Do not be afraid, little flock, for your Father has been pleased to give you the kingdom. Sell your possessions and give to the poor. Provide purses for yourselves that will not wear out, a treasure in heaven that will not be exhausted, where no thief comes near and no moth destroys. For where your treasure is, there your heart will be also" (Luke 12:32–34).

If our Father has been pleased to give us His kingdom, can we fail to be as generous? Are we to take Jesus literally at His word and actually sell all our possessions? Should we literally give to everyone who asks?

Francis of Assisi, the son of a cloth merchant in medieval Italy, took Jesus literally and gave away everything he owned. Few of us can imagine abandoning our middle-class lifestyles to become voluntarily homeless like Francis. And since Jesus didn't require that of all His followers, He probably doesn't require it of us.

Rabbis of Jesus' day often used hyperbole, or extreme exaggeration, to get their points across. So maybe we don't have to give away *everything* to *everyone* who asks for it. But neither can we dismiss Jesus' instructions as mere exaggeration. He is making a point. The question is, what is His point, and how does it apply to us?

2. What do you feel when you read Jesus' words from Luke 6 and 12 above?

3. How do you think Jesus' words, "*Give to everyone who asks you, and if anyone takes what belongs to you, do not demand it back. Do to others as you would have them do to you,*" apply to Carol and Jeff's situation?

4. What reasons for being generous does Jesus give in Luke 6 and 12?

5. How would you summarize the point(s) Jesus is making in these two passages?

6. What do you think Jesus wants us to do with His instruction, "*Sell your possessions and give to the poor*"?

7. Do you struggle with when to be generous and when to keep your time or money for your own needs? Describe one such struggle.

Any of the attitudes we have discussed in previous sessions can complicate our efforts to become generous. Remember Shelly from session 3? She thinks she has to ensure her own needs, present and future, are taken care of before she can afford to be generous. She will likely find it hard to be genuinely generous until she confronts her fear that God will not provide for her. Shelly's stinginess is rooted in fear. Pride or greed might be the root of another person's selfishness.

Either money will rule Shelly, or she will learn to rule money and let God rule her. At some point she will have to decide whether her first priority is storing treasure on earth or storing it in heaven. Because her heart is wherever her treasure is, she will find that generosity rarely wells up from her heart until she has begun to shift her priorities.

Money is never "just money"; it is constantly propelling us either deeper into a partnership with God or deeper into our self-centeredness. As we evaluate our attitudes in light of the values of God's kingdom, we sense the Spirit of God drawing us beyond the worship of mammon to the worship of God; beyond worry to faith; beyond greed and pride to humility, contentment, gratitude, justice, and finally an openhearted generosity. We begin to gain God's perspective that neighbors far outweigh things, and treasure in heaven is far more valuable than treasure on earth.

8. Take a few minutes to assess what you've learned from this study. What new ideas or perspectives have you gained?

9. How has this study affected the way you've been viewing and treating money during the past few weeks?

10. Where would you like to go from here with what you've learned?

The Grace Adventure

We won't shift from fear and pride to gratitude and generosity overnight, but we can take the next step on our spiritual walk, knowing that God's Spirit is at work in us.

11. Give group participants an opportunity to either thank God for what they have learned or ask for wisdom about a particular issue. Close by asking God to help you live in an attitude of gratitude and generosity.

During the Week

- Review the verses you have been focusing on during this study. What has the Holy Spirit revealed in them that you didn't see when you started?

* * * *

"Command those who are rich in this present world not to be arrogant nor to put their hope in wealth, which is so uncertain, but to put their hope in God, who richly provides us with everything for our enjoyment. Command them to do good, to be rich in good deeds, and to be generous and willing to share. In this way they will lay up treasures for themselves as a firm foundation for the coming age, so that they may take hold of the life that is truly life" (1 Timothy 6:17–19).

Larry Burkett, founder and president of Christian Financial Concepts, is the best-selling author of 37 books on business and personal finances and 2 novels. He also hosts two radio programs broadcast on hundreds of stations worldwide.

Larry holds degrees in marketing and finance, and for several years served as a manager in the space program at Cape Canaveral, Florida. He also has been vice president of an electronics manufacturing firm. Larry's education, business experience, and solid understanding of God's Word enable him to give practical, Bible-based financial counsel to families, churches, and businesses.

Founded in 1976, Christian Financial Concepts is a nonprofit, nondenominational ministry dedicated to helping God's people gain a clear understanding of how to manage their money according to scriptural principles. While practical assistance is provided on many levels, the purpose of CFC is simply *to bring glory to God by freeing His people from financial bondage so they may serve Him to their utmost*.

One major avenue of ministry involves the training of volunteers in budget and debt counseling and linking them with financially troubled families and individuals through a nationwide referral network. CFC also provides financial management seminars and workshops for churches and other groups. (Formats available include audio, video, video with moderator, and live instruction.) A full line of printed and audio-visual materials related to money management is available through CFC's materials department (1-800-722-1976).

Career Pathways, another outreach of Christian Financial Concepts, helps teenagers and adults find their occupational calling. The Career Pathways "Testing Package" gauges a person's work priorities, skills, vocational interests, and personality. Reports in each of these areas define a person's strengths, weaknesses, and unique, God-given pattern for work.

For further information about the ministry of Christian Financial Concepts, write to:

Christian Financial Concepts
PO Box 2377
Gainesville, GA 30503-2377

OTHER BOOKS BY LARRY BURKETT
Available at your local bookstore

The Financial Planning Workbook

This workbook includes practical advice about managing your finances and provides a series of easy-to-follow worksheets that allow you to structure and maintain your family's budget. Larry shows you where to start, how to stay on track, and even addresses special budgeting problems. Extra worksheets are included.

The Word on Finances

This useful tool contains a collection of relevant Scriptures arranged under eight comprehensive headings. Larry's practical wisdom opens each of the more than seventy topical selections.

Debt-Free Living

This book is for anyone whose money ran out before the month did. Again. Or even if your financial situation hasn't reached a crisis point, you will benefit from Larry's wise counsel. Through case studies of several marriages helped through proper financial counsel, Larry shows how to become and remain debt-free. He warns about the kinds of credit to avoid and provides specific how-to's for solving debt problems. *Debt-Free Living* remains a best-seller, with more than 150,000 copies in print.

How to Manage Your Money

There is so much religious "folklore" regarding money that few Christians understand God's true will in finances. But the Scriptures have plenty to say about how we should handle the funds entrusted to us. There are more than 700 direct references to money in the Bible and hundreds more indirect references. *How to Manage Your Money*, a Bible study by Larry Burkett, brings many of these references to light as it introduces Christians to the "scriptural" view of finances. This workbook covers such topics as stewardship, short- and long-range planning, tithing, and much more.

Your Finances in Changing Times

With more than a million copies in print, this book is a perfect introduction to basic financial management. It is a complete money guide, offering biblical concepts and practical suggestions for building a sound financial program. Learn to plan for the future, get out or stay out of debt, and much more.

Moody Press, a ministry of the Moody Bible Institute,
is designed for education, evangelization, and edification.
If we may assist you in knowing more about Christ
and the Christian life, please write us without obligation:
Moody Press, c/o MLM, Chicago, Illinois 60610.